GROUNDBREAKER BIOS

Amelia Earhart

BY KATE CONLEY

CONTENT CONSULTANT
DOROTHY S. COCHRANE
CURATOR, GENERAL AVIATION & AERONAUTICS DEPARTMENT
NATIONAL AIR AND SPACE MUSEUM

Kids Core
An Imprint of Abdo Publishing
abdobooks.com

abdobooks.com

Published by Abdo Publishing, a division of ABDO, PO Box 398166, Minneapolis, Minnesota 55439.

Printed in the United States of America, North Mankato, Minnesota.
102021
012022

THIS BOOK CONTAINS RECYCLED MATERIALS

Cover Photo: picture-alliance/dpa/AP Images
Interior Photos: Bettmann/Getty Images, 4–5; B Christopher/Alamy, 6, 28 (left); Keystone Pictures USA/Zuma Press/Alamy, 8; AP Images, 10–11, 18–19, 20, 24, 28 (right), 29 (top); Carlos Osorio/Toronto Star/Getty Images, 12; George Rinhart/Corbis Historical/Getty Images, 14; PictureLux/The Hollywood Archive/Alamy, 15; Science History Images/Alamy, 16; Everett Collection/Shutterstock Images, 22, 26, 29 (bottom); Red Line Editorial, 25

Editor: Ann Schwab
Series Designer: Christine Ha

Library of Congress Control Number: 2021941511

Publisher's Cataloging-in-Publication Data

Names: Conley, Kate, author.
Title: Amelia Earhart / by Kate Conley
Description: Minneapolis, Minnesota : Abdo Publishing, 2022 | Series: Groundbreaker bios | Includes online resources and index.
Identifiers: ISBN 9781532196836 (lib. bdg.) | ISBN 9781644946671 (pbk.) | ISBN 9781098218645 (ebook)
Subjects: LCSH: Earhart, Amelia, 1897-1937--Juvenile literature. | Air pilots--United States--Biography--Juvenile literature. | Women air pilots--United States--Biography--Juvenile literature. | Women in aeronautics--Biography--Juvenile literature. | Missing persons--Biography--Juvenile literature.
Classification: DDC 629.13092 [B]--dc23

CONTENTS

Amelia Earhart paved the way for future female pilots.

CHAPTER 1

Discovering Flight

At age 23, Amelia Earhart and her father visited an **airfield** near Los Angeles, California. They watched pilots race and perform tricks. The pilots drew huge crowds. Flying was an exciting, new way to travel.

As a young girl, Amelia enjoyed outdoor adventures.

Earhart was captivated by what she saw. She wanted to try flying.

The next day, Earhart took her first plane ride. The pilot circled over Los Angeles. Then he made a pass over the Pacific Ocean. When they landed, Earhart knew she wanted to become a pilot. She quickly began lessons. Her flight career had begun.

Young Thrill Seeker

Amelia Earhart was born on July 24, 1897, in Atchison, Kansas. She lived with her parents and her younger sister. As a child, Amelia loved to read and play outside.

When Amelia was seven, her family took a trip. They went to the World's Fair in Saint Louis, Missouri. Amelia enjoyed riding the Ferris wheel.

The Wright Brothers

The brothers Orville and Wilbur Wright were interested in flight. They wanted to build an airplane powered by a motor. It took years of trial and error. They succeeded on December 17, 1903. That day they made the first powered flight in history that was manned, controlled, and heavier-than-air.

The 1904 World's Fair in Saint Louis featured an automobile parade and a Ferris wheel.

She loved being high in the air. Amelia wanted to try the roller coaster too, but her mother said no.

At home, Amelia built her own roller coaster. She propped boards against a shed. They served as the tracks. Then she attached wheels to a wooden crate. It became the car. The ride provided a thrill that Amelia would chase for the rest of her life.

Explore Online

Watch the short video on the website below. Does it give you any new information about the role Amelia Earhart and other women played in the history of flight?

Pioneering Women in Early Aviation

abdocorelibrary.com/amelia-earhart

Ogontz students, including Earhart, took graduation photos early in the school year. But Earhart decided to leave school before graduation.

CHAPTER 2

Fascination with Flight

In 1915, Earhart graduated from high school in Chicago. She then went to the Ogontz School in Pennsylvania. In December 1917, Earhart traveled to Toronto, Canada. She visited her sister, who was studying there.

During World War I, Earhart worked at the Spadina Military Hospital in Toronto, Canada.

In Toronto, Earhart saw many soldiers who had been wounded in World War I (1914–1918). She wanted to help them. So she left school to volunteer as a nurse's aide at a military hospital.

One day Earhart went to the local airfield. There, she got her first up-close view of a modern airplane. Earhart wanted to fly, but it was not possible. The pilots were all members of the military. **Civilians** could not go up in the planes. Earhart did the next best thing. She started spending her free time at the airfield. She learned as much as she could about flying.

Earhart and Women's Rights

Amelia Earhart was a believer in equal rights for women. She felt women should have the same opportunities for education and jobs as men. Earhart helped create the Ninety-Nines, an organization for female pilots. It is still in existence today.

Learning to Fly

After the war, Earhart returned to the United States. She enrolled at Columbia University in New York. Earhart planned to be a doctor, but she left college after a year. She moved to California where her parents were living.

There, she visited the air show with her father. And she then began to pursue her dream.

Air shows in the 1920s featured many tricks and stunts.

In her early 20s, Earhart considered a career in medicine before focusing on becoming a pilot.

Once Earhart began flying, she bought her own plane as soon as she could.

On December 28, 1920, Earhart rode in an airplane for the first time. Just days later, on January 3, 1921, she began flying lessons.

Within months, she bought a small, fast **biplane**. Earhart called it the *Canary* because it was bright yellow. In 1923, she earned her pilot's license. Earhart soon began flying in women's races and air shows.

Further Evidence

Look at the website below. Does it give any new evidence to help support the ideas in Chapter Two?

History of Aircraft

abdocorelibrary.com/amelia-earhart

After crossing the Atlantic on *Friendship*, Earhart was greeted as a hero.

CHAPTER 3

Flying Hero

In May 1928, Earhart joined the crew of the *Friendship.* They left from Canada and flew across the Atlantic Ocean. Then they landed in Wales. On this flight, Earhart became the first woman to fly over the Atlantic Ocean.

In 1932, Earhart made history as the first woman to fly solo across the Atlantic Ocean. A huge crowd gathered to wish her well on her return trip.

People saw Earhart as a hero. The praise made Earhart uneasy. She had not piloted the plane during the trip. She had only kept the flight log. But that didn't matter. Earhart became an instant celebrity. She gave speeches to groups across the country about her flight.

Earhart wanted to fly across the Atlantic again. But this time she wanted to be the pilot. On May 20, 1932, she took off from Newfoundland, Canada. She landed in Northern Ireland 15 hours later. She had become the first woman to fly **solo** across the Atlantic Ocean.

20 Hours and 40 Minutes

Earhart wrote a best-selling book about the *Friendship* flight. It was called *20 Hours and 40 Minutes*. G. P. Putnam published the book. As they worked on it, Earhart and Putnam fell in love. They married in 1931.

Earhart waves to her fans after her coast-to-coast flight across the United States in 1932. It was the first time a woman had made that solo flight.

Earhart continued to break records. In August 1932, she became the first woman to make a solo, nonstop flight across the United States. She flew from California to New Jersey in just over 19 hours. In January 1935, she became the first person to fly solo from Hawaii to California.

Final Flight

Earhart's next big goal was to fly around the world. Starting from Oakland, California, the trip would cover 29,000 miles (47,000 km). She would fly as close to the **equator** as possible. A **navigator**, Fred Noonan, joined her. On June 1, 1937, they took off from Miami, Florida, to start the next **leg** of the trip.

Earhart and her navigator, Fred Noonan, review a map of the Pacific Ocean in preparation for their trip around the world.

By July 2, they had already flown 22,000 miles (35,400 km). The next leg of the trip was dangerous. They had to cross the Pacific Ocean. Earhart and Noonan planned to

In 1937, Amelia Earhart attempted to become the first female pilot to fly around the world. This map shows the flight path of her doomed journey and some of the stops along the route. How does this map help you better understand her final trip?

refuel on Howland Island. But they had trouble finding the tiny island.

Earhart's bravery and adventurous spirit continue to inspire people today.

Earhart and Noonan never arrived at Howland Island. Despite many searches, they were never found. What happened to them remains a mystery. Most experts believe that the plane ran out of fuel and crashed into the Pacific Ocean. In the years since then, Earhart has become a legend. People admire her bravery and daring spirit during the early years of flight.

Primary Source

Earhart's flights were difficult. She had a close call during her 1932 solo flight over the Atlantic. She later wrote how she almost crashed into the ocean:

> The plane suddenly "iced up" and went into a spin. How long we spun I do not know. As we righted and held level again, through the blackness below I could see the white-caps [of the waves] too close for comfort.

Source: Amelia Earhart. *Last Flight.* Harcourt, Brace, 1937, p. 18.

What's the Big Idea?

Read this quote carefully. What is its main idea? Explain how the main idea is supported by details.

Timeline

1897
Amelia Earhart is born in Atchison, Kansas, on July 24.

1920
Earhart takes her first ride in an airplane.

1921
Earhart begins flying lessons.

1928
While aboard the *Friendship*, Earhart is the first woman to fly over the Atlantic Ocean.

1937
Earhart attempts to fly around the world, but her plane disappears over the Pacific Ocean on July 2.

1932
In May Earhart is the first woman to fly solo over the Atlantic Ocean, and in August she is the first woman to fly solo, nonstop, across the United States.

1935
Earhart is the first person to fly solo from Hawaii to California.

Glossary

airfield
an area of land from which aircraft operate

biplane
an airplane that has two sets of wings that are stacked on top of each other

civilians
people who are not part of the military

equator
an imaginary line that divides a globe into north and south and is equally distant from the north and south poles

leg
in describing a journey, a specific distance of the trip

navigator
someone who accurately plots a person's place along a route

solo
something done by a single person

Online Resources

To learn more about Amelia Earhart, visit our free resource websites below.

Core Library CONNECTION
FREE! COMMON CORE MULTIMEDIA RESOURCES

Visit **abdocorelibrary.com** or scan this QR code for free Common Core resources for teachers and students, including vetted activities, multimedia, and booklinks, for deeper subject comprehension.

Booklinks NONFICTION NETWORK
FREE! ONLINE NONFICTION RESOURCES

Visit **abdobooklinks.com** or scan this QR code for free additional online weblinks for further learning. These links are routinely monitored and updated to provide the most current information available.

Learn More

Buckley, James, Jr. *Amelia Earhart: Pioneer of the Sky!* Portable, 2018.

Morgan, Sally. *Amelia Earhart: First Woman over the Atlantic.* Random House, 2021.

Index

About the Author

Kate Conley has been writing nonfiction books for children for more than ten years. When she's not writing, Conley spends her time reading, sewing, and solving crossword puzzles. She lives in Minnesota with her husband and two children.